Why Does Mum Wear A Hijab?

written by
Amal Abou-Eid

Illustrated by
Samira Abou-Eid

Why Does Mum Wear A Hijab?

Copyright © Amal Abou-Eid
Illustration Copyright © Samira Abou-Eid

First Edition 2019

All rights reserved. No part of this book may be reproduced or transmitted in any form or by any means, electronic, mechanical, photocopying or otherwise without prior permission of the publisher.

ISBN 978-0-6487113-9-1

For mum,

Because you always know.

It was a cold winter's day in Melbourne. Maryam sat by the window watching the rain fall. She wanted to play outside but everything was wet. 'I hate being stuck inside. I don't think this rain will ever stop,' she moaned.

'Quit whinging, Maryam. Go and find something to do,' said her big sister Amina, as she pulled out her sketchpad.

Amina was happy to be indoors. She was very artistic and loved sitting at her desk, sketching and drawing all kinds of things. She drew pictures of unicorns, fairies and witches but her favourite thing to draw was her family.

Whenever she drew her family, she would draw her dad looking smart and handsome with his black beard and glasses. She would draw her little sister, Maryam, wearing colourful dresses with ribbons in her hair.

But before she would draw her mum, she would stop and think about her *hijab*. Should she draw her with or without it? Should her clothes be the ones she wore at home or the ones she wore when she was out and about?

No matter how much she thought about it, she would always draw her mum wearing her *hijab*.

She knew the *hijab* was important to her, she just didn't understand why.

That morning, as the rain fell heavily outside, Amina sat at her desk and drew a picture of her parents. She drew her dad's beard and glasses as usual, but, for the first time, she drew her mum without her *hijab*. When she finished her drawing, she showed it to her mum.

'What a lovely picture of your dad and me,' said her mum. 'But where is my *hijab*?'

'You don't wear it when you're at home,' said Amina, looking at her mum. 'Why do you wear a *hijab*?'

Her mum smiled and said, 'There are lots of reasons why I choose to wear my *hijab*. It is part of my identity as a Muslim woman. The *hijab* is an expression of my faith and my obedience to God.'

'So, you wear it as a symbol of your faith?' asked Amina.

'Yes, that's right. People of other religions and beliefs express themselves in other ways. Our Jewish neighbour wears a *kippah*. Your Christian teacher wears a *cross*. Some people wear tunics or robes…'

'My best friend's dad wears a turban!' exclaimed Amina.

'That's called a *dastaar* and is usually worn by Sikh men. People choose to worship and express their faith in ways that make them comfortable,' explained her mum.

'That makes sense, mum. So why doesn't dad wear a *hijab* too? asked Amina.

'Muslim men are encouraged to grow their beards like prophet Muhammad peace be upon him and must wear modest and loose clothing.'

'Some Muslim men wear traditional hats, like your grandad's *kufi*. Muslims around the world express themselves in many ways and style their *hijabs* and hats differently,' said her mum.

'Do you like to wear the *hijab*?' asked Amina.

'Yes, my darling. It is my precious crown. It gives me honour and dignity and shows the world I am a Muslim queen,' replied her mum proudly.

'And on days like today, your hair will stay dry in the rain!' giggled Amina.

She thanked her mum and went back to her desk to draw another picture.

Amina's chat with her mum helped her to understand the significance of the *hijab*, the beard and other religious symbols. They were simply representations of a person's faith and their connection to God.

The next day, Amina woke up feeling inspired. She wanted to wear a *hijab* to school.

Plain, colourful, floral and sparkly; her mum had so many *hijabs* to choose from. Amina picked one that matched her school uniform and wore it on her head.

'Surprise!' shouted Amina, as she walked into the kitchen.

'Masha'Allah darling, the *hijab* looks beautiful on you!' said her mum cheerfully.

'Your friends might not recognise you, but I think you look lovely,' said her dad.

'Thank you. Today, I will wear a *hijab* to school because I am a Muslim and the *hijab* is my crown,' Amina announced.

'I want to wear a crown, too!' giggled Maryam and ran off to get herself a *hijab*.

Amina sat beside her mum and gave her a piece of paper.

'I drew this for you, mum.' It was a picture of them together, both wearing a *hijab*, proudly.

Amina's mum wears a *hijab* because she is a Muslim. When she wears her *hijab*, she feels like a Queen!
Do you have something special you like to wear?

Glossary

Cross: a symbol of Jesus Christ worn by people of the Christian faith.

Dastaar: A hat that resembles a turban, made out of draped fabric, worn by people of the Sikh faith.

Hijab: a head covering/veil worn by women of the Islamic faith.

Islam: monotheistic religion of Muslims. Muslims believe in one God (Allah) and the final messenger prophet Muhammad peace be upon him.

Kippah: a small hat or skullcap worn by people of the Jewish faith.

Kufi: brimless, small and rounded cap worn mostly by African and Asian men.

Masha'Allah: an Arabic phrase often translated as 'God has willed' used to express appreciation, joy, praise, or thankfulness.

Peace Be Upon Him: an expression used after mentioning prophet Muhammad as a sign of respect and honour.

A Muslim Woman's Hijab

A poem by Amal Abou-Eid

A Muslim woman's hijab is a gift from the Almighty, sent down to protect and honour her.

It is a declaration of her faith and her submission to the command of her Lord.

Her hijab is her uniform reminding her to be considerate with her actions and words.

She is a representative of Islam. She must wear this honour proudly.

A Muslim woman's hijab is her crown and her glory. It gives her pride and dignity.

She is a queen; with that comes an enormous amount of strength, power and fragility.

It is her protection from wandering eyes and her sanctuary from the evils of this world.

The hijab gives a woman her value and her worth. It is her way of telling the world it does not matter what I look like, what matters is what I say and how I think.

It is an expression of modesty, decency and respect. An affirmation that she is not an object.

She is more.

A lot more.

A Muslim woman's hijab is her liberty and her freedom.

It empowers her and raises her and reminds her she has been blessed with a gift from her Lord; and for that she is thankful.

About the Author

AMAL ABOU-EID is a passionate educator and very busy mother to 3 young boys. Living in Melbourne, Australia, Amal is surrounded by people of various faiths and cultures.

The daughter of Lebanese migrants, Amal identifies as a Muslim Lebanese Australian and credits the splendours of multiculturalism as her inspiration for writing.

Hoping to educate readers about her faith and her cultural heritage, Amal writes books which explain aspects of Islam that are often misunderstood and misrepresented.

She hopes her books will give Muslim children stories they can relate to and stories they can identify with. She hopes her stories will educate readers and inspire others to share their own stories, too.

Her first book 'My Muslim Mate' was well received by Muslims and non-Muslims alike. Be sure to check it out at www.booksbyamal.com.au

www.ingramcontent.com/pod-product-compliance
Lightning Source LLC
Chambersburg PA
CBHW041429010526
44107CB00045B/1545